Worship Now, Worship Forever

A Journey from Earthly Praise to Eternal Glory

Gerard Assey

Table of Contents

Preface

Worship is far more than a mere ritual, a routine act of devotion. It is the very expression of our souls reaching out to the divine—an act that mirrors what is happening in heaven at this very moment. The title of this book, **'Worship Now, Worship Forever: *A Journey from Earthly Praise to Eternal Glory*'**, encapsulates this profound reality. As we worship here on earth, we are rehearsing for the eternal worship we will offer to God in His presence for all eternity.

In this book, we explore worship not just as an earthly duty but as a divine calling. From the breath of life God first gave us (Genesis 2:7) to the moment when every knee will bow and every tongue confess that Jesus Christ is Lord (Philippians 2:10-11), worship defines our relationship with God. It prepares us, both individually and as the collective Body of Christ, for the ultimate reality of being with Him forever.

Drawing from Scripture, stories from both the Old and New Testaments, and real-life examples, this book will take you through the essential elements of worship. It will show you how our every action, thought, and emotion can become part of an ongoing symphony of praise that aligns our hearts with heaven. Together, we will explore the journey from our daily worship to the eternal celebration we are destined to partake in before God's throne.

As you turn the pages of this book, may you discover how to live a life of worship that reflects heaven's reality here and now, knowing that every act of praise today is a step closer to the eternal glory we will experience forever.

Worship as a Heavenly Rehearsal

Worship is often perceived as a form of expressing reverence and devotion to God. But in the Christian faith, it carries a deeper, more profound significance. Worship on earth is not merely an act of praise; it is a preparation—a dress rehearsal—for the eternal worship that believers will engage in when they stand in the presence of God in heaven. As Christians, when we gather to worship, we are participating in an earthly reflection of a heavenly reality. The eternal praise, adoration, and glorification of God that takes place in the heavenly realms serve as the ultimate example of what worship should be like on earth.

Worship as a Glimpse of Eternity

The idea of worship as a rehearsal for heaven is not just a metaphor but a scriptural truth. In **Revelation 5:11-14**, John gives us a powerful vision of worship in heaven. He describes an innumerable multitude of angels and every living creature bowing down before the Lamb, saying, *"Worthy is the Lamb who was slain, to receive power and wealth and wisdom and might and honor and glory and blessing!"* This passage shows us that worship is central to the heavenly existence and that it will be the main occupation of believers in eternity. The angels and saints in heaven are perpetually engaged in the act of glorifying God, and this heavenly worship offers a blueprint for how we should approach worship while we are still here on earth.

The vision in Revelation reveals the scale and intensity of worship in heaven. It is not a passive or half-hearted activity but an all-consuming, joyful, and reverent acknowledgment of God's greatness. Every knee bows, every voice is raised, and the full assembly of heaven praises the Lord with one voice. Worship on earth, therefore, is not only a time of communion with God but also a spiritual training ground, preparing our hearts, minds, and spirits for this future reality.

Worship as Practice for Heaven

If we consider worship on earth as a rehearsal, we can think of it as practicing for the grandest performance of our lives. Just as musicians rehearse for a concert or actors prepare for a play, believers engage in worship to ready themselves for the day when they will worship God face to face. This analogy is deeply rooted in the scriptural emphasis on the communal and continual nature of worship, both now and in the life to come.

In the **Old Testament**, worship was often seen in the structured and sacred rituals of temple life. **Psalm 100:4** encourages believers to *"Enter his gates with thanksgiving, and his courts with praise,"* which hints at the idea of approaching God's presence with intentionality and reverence. The rituals of temple worship—the sacrifices, the songs, the prayers—were designed not just as acts of devotion but as a way to cultivate the discipline and mindset needed to honor God in a manner worthy of His holiness. These acts were physical rehearsals for a spiritual reality that would be fully realized in the New Jerusalem, where God will dwell with His people forever (Revelation 21:3).

Old Testament: Worship as Preparation for God's Presence

The **Old Testament** is rich with examples of how worship was intended to prepare God's people for His presence. One of the most notable examples is found in the construction of the **Tabernacle** during the time of Moses. In **Exodus 25-30**, God provides Moses with very specific instructions on how to build the Tabernacle, where Israel would worship. The Tabernacle was not just a physical structure; it was a place where God's presence would dwell among His people. Every item in the Tabernacle—from the Ark of the Covenant to the altar of incense—had symbolic meaning and pointed to heavenly realities. Hebrews 8:5 explains that these things served as *"a copy and shadow of the heavenly things."* The worship conducted in the Tabernacle was a direct precursor to the worship that would take place in heaven.

Worship, in the Old Testament sense, was deeply connected to the idea of God's holiness and the people's need to be prepared to encounter Him. The rituals of sacrifice and purification were not just about following rules; they were about teaching the people how to honor and approach a holy God. Similarly, our acts of worship today—whether through singing, prayer, or acts of service—prepare us to encounter God in His fullness.

New Testament: Worship in Spirit and Truth

In the **New Testament**, worship takes on a more intimate and personal dimension with the coming of Jesus Christ. In **John 4:23-24**, Jesus tells the Samaritan woman that *"the hour is coming, and is now here, when the true worshipers will worship the Father in spirit and truth, for the Father is seeking such people to worship him. God is spirit, and those who worship him must worship in spirit and truth."* This passage highlights the fact that earthly worship is not just about external rituals but about the posture of our hearts. It's about aligning our spirits with the truth of who God is.

Jesus's conversation with the Samaritan woman also hints at the idea that worship is not confined to a particular place or time; rather, it is a continuous expression of love and devotion to God. This is a crucial aspect of worship as a rehearsal for heaven. In heaven, worship is not bound by time, space, or form—it is a perpetual state of being. As believers, we are called to enter into this continuous state of worship now, living lives that reflect the glory and greatness of God in everything we do.

The **New Testament church** provides a model for how worship prepares believers for heaven. In **Acts 2:42-47**, the early Christians devoted themselves to the apostles' teaching, fellowship, breaking of bread, and prayer. Their worship was not just a Sunday activity; it was a way of life that shaped their entire community. This communal worship was a reflection of the heavenly community where all believers will worship God together. In their gathering, sharing, and praising, the early Christians were rehearsing for the eternal fellowship they would one day experience in God's presence.

Real-Life Application: Worship as Life's Grand Rehearsal

In practical terms, the idea of worship as a rehearsal for heaven can change the way we approach our times of worship here on earth. Consider the structure of a Sunday service in many churches: there is often a time of praise through music, prayers of confession and thanksgiving, a sermon, and a closing act of blessing or benediction. Each of these elements mirrors, in some way, the scenes of worship described in heaven. The praise songs reflect the unceasing worship of the angels. The confession and thanksgiving remind us of our dependence on God's grace and mercy, much like the saints in heaven who acknowledge the Lamb who was slain for their redemption. The sermon is an opportunity to hear the Word of God, just as we will experience divine revelation in His presence. Finally, the benediction serves as a reminder of God's blessing and protection, which will be fully realized in eternity.

But worship is not limited to a church service. **Romans 12:1** calls believers to offer their bodies as living sacrifices, holy and pleasing to God, which is described as *"true and proper worship."* This means that every act of obedience, service, love, and devotion in our daily lives is a form of worship. Just as rehearsals prepare performers for the final event, these daily acts of worship are preparing us for the ultimate worship experience in heaven.

In real life, worshipping God in the mundane tasks of life is like practicing for the ultimate reality. Whether it's through work, family life, or personal struggles, believers are called to glorify God in everything they do. This prepares their hearts for the moment when they will join the great heavenly choir in worshiping God for all eternity.

Earthly Worship, Heavenly Reality

In summary, worship on earth is a profound rehearsal for the eternal worship that will take place in heaven. The **Old Testament** teaches us that worship is a sacred practice, preparing us to meet a holy God, while the **New Testament** emphasizes worship in spirit and truth as an ongoing, intimate relationship with God. Revelation gives us a clear picture of the grandeur and intensity of heavenly worship, and every act of worship on earth is a step toward that ultimate reality. As believers, we are invited to live lives of continual worship, preparing our hearts and spirits for the eternal worship that awaits us in the presence of God.

The Purpose of Worship on Earth

Worship on earth is an essential and transformative aspect of the Christian life, but its significance stretches far beyond our present experience. It serves not only as an act of devotion but also as a divine preparation for eternity. As Christians, we are called to understand the deeper purpose behind worship, recognizing that our earthly worship is a mirror image of what takes place in heaven. In this chapter, we will explore why worship is vital, how it prepares us for eternity, and what Scripture reveals about the eternal nature of worship.

The Divine Purpose of Worship

At its core, worship is about honoring, revering, and glorifying God. It is an act that acknowledges God's sovereignty, majesty, and holiness, while reminding us of our dependence on Him. Worship, however, is not centered on us; it is about God. It draws our hearts, minds, and spirits away from our own desires and onto God's character and His glory. In **Revelation 4:10-11**, we see this heavenly reality in full display. The twenty-four elders fall down before the throne of God, casting their crowns at His feet, and proclaiming, *"Worthy are you, our Lord and God, to receive glory and honor and power, for you created all things, and by your will they existed and were created."* This passage highlights the fundamental truth of worship: it is an expression of the worthiness of God, who deserves all glory.

Our worship on earth is meant to reflect this heavenly worship. The elders' act of casting their crowns is a powerful symbol of submission, recognizing that all honor and authority ultimately belong to God. In our own lives, worship serves as a continual reminder that God is in control, and we are His creation, dependent upon Him for everything. By participating in worship, we align ourselves with the reality of God's dominion and prepare our hearts for the eternal worship we will experience in heaven.

Old Testament Example: The Tabernacle Worship
In the **Old Testament**, worship was deeply connected to the concept of holiness and God's presence. One of the most significant examples of this is the worship conducted in the Tabernacle. God gave the Israelites specific instructions for building the Tabernacle, which would serve as the place where His presence would dwell among His people.

In **Exodus 25:8**, God says, *"And let them make me a sanctuary, that I may dwell in their midst."* The Tabernacle was not just a physical structure; it was a sacred space where God's holiness would be made manifest, and the people could approach Him through worship and sacrifice.

In **Hebrews 8:5**, the author of Hebrews explains that the Tabernacle and its worship rituals were *"a copy and shadow of the heavenly things."* This reveals that the worship conducted in the Tabernacle was a physical reflection of the eternal worship that takes place in heaven. The sacrifices, offerings, and rituals were all designed to point to greater spiritual truths about God's holiness and His plan for salvation. These acts of worship were not ends in themselves but served to prepare the people for a deeper understanding of God's nature and His redemptive work.

The worship in the Tabernacle was structured, intentional, and centered on God's presence. The priests would enter into the Holy of Holies, where the

Ark of the Covenant was kept, to offer sacrifices and prayers on behalf of the people. This sacred act of worship foreshadowed the access that believers would one day have through Jesus Christ, who serves as the ultimate High Priest (Hebrews 9:11). In the same way that the Israelites' worship was a preparation for God's presence, our worship today prepares us for the eternal worship we will experience in heaven.

New Testament Example: Worship in Spirit and Truth

In the **New Testament**, Jesus introduces a profound shift in the understanding of worship. In His conversation with the Samaritan woman at the well, Jesus explains that true worship is not about a specific place or ritual but about the heart. In **John 4:23-24**, He says, *"But the hour is coming, and is now here, when the true worshipers will worship the Father in spirit and truth, for the Father is seeking such people to worship him. God is spirit, and those who worship him must worship in spirit and truth."*

This teaching emphasizes the spiritual nature of worship. While the Old Testament worship practices were centered on physical sacrifices and rituals, Jesus reveals that the essence of worship lies in the heart's posture toward God. Worship in spirit and truth means that we must engage with God authentically, with sincerity and reverence, recognizing His holiness and our need for His grace. This type of worship transcends time and space, preparing us for the eternal worship in heaven where we will stand before God in perfect communion.

Jesus' call to worship in spirit and truth also reflects the unity that believers will experience in heaven. In heaven, worship will not be divided by denominations, cultures, or traditions. There will be no barriers between us and God or between believers. The earthly divisions that sometimes characterize our worship will be dissolved in the presence of God, where we will worship Him together as one body. This vision of unity should inspire us to seek greater harmony in our worship here on earth, as we anticipate the day when we will join the multitudes in heaven, proclaiming God's glory with one voice.

Real-Life Example: Corporate Worship as a Rehearsal for Heaven

One of the most tangible ways we experience the purpose of worship on earth is through corporate worship. When the church gathers to worship, we are practicing for the unity, harmony, and glorification that will take place in heaven. In a sense, each Sunday service is a mini-rehearsal for the eternal worship we will participate in when we stand before God's throne.

Imagine a choir preparing for a grand performance. Each rehearsal is an opportunity for the choir to refine their skills, harmonize their voices, and ensure that every member is aligned with the conductor's direction. In the same way, corporate worship allows believers to come together, lift their voices in praise, and practice the kind of unity and harmony that will be fully realized in heaven. Every song sung, every prayer offered, and every Scripture read is a reminder that we are part of something much bigger than ourselves. We are part of the body of Christ, rehearsing for the day when we will worship Him eternally.

In our daily lives, worship can also take many forms. Whether it's through music, prayer, service, or simply living in obedience to God's will, each act of worship draws us closer to Him and prepares our hearts for the eternal worship we will experience in heaven. For example, a Christian mother singing hymns while doing household chores is worshipping God through her daily tasks. A businessman who chooses to conduct his business ethically, with integrity and love for others, is worshiping God through his work. These seemingly small acts of worship are, in reality, profound rehearsals for the day when all of creation will glorify God together.

Worship as Our Eternal Destiny
The purpose of worship on earth is to glorify God and to prepare us for our eternal destiny. In both the **Old Testament** and **New Testament**, we see how worship serves as a reflection of heavenly realities, pointing us toward the day when we will stand before God in perfect communion. Worship is not about us; it is about God. It is a response to His greatness, His love, and His worthiness.

As believers, we are called to engage in worship with intentionality, recognizing that every act of praise, every song, and every prayer is a step closer to the eternal worship we will experience in heaven. Whether in corporate worship or in our daily lives, worship is a divine rehearsal, preparing our hearts for the day when we will join the multitudes in proclaiming, *"Worthy are you, our Lord and God, to receive glory and honor and power"* (Revelation 4:11).

Let us worship with hearts full of anticipation, knowing that our earthly worship is but a shadow of the glorious worship that awaits us in heaven.

The Heavenly Model of Worship

When we think of worship in heaven, we often envision a scene of awe, reverence, and eternal praise. The Bible offers us glimpses of heavenly worship that can stir our spirits and guide our worship on earth. Understanding the heavenly model of worship helps us align our hearts with the eternal purpose of glorifying God. Worship in heaven is not momentary or sporadic; it is constant, filled with an overwhelming sense of God's presence, and it transcends all human limitations. In this chapter, we will explore how heavenly worship is portrayed in Scripture, through both Old and New Testament examples, and how it serves as the ultimate pattern for our worship here on earth.

The Heavenly Scene: Revelation 7:9-12

In **Revelation 7:9-12**, the Apostle John is given a magnificent vision of the multitudes worshiping before the throne of God. John describes a scene where *"a great multitude that no one could count, from every nation, tribe, people, and language, standing before the throne and before the Lamb"* are worshiping. These people are clothed in white robes, holding palm branches, and crying out with loud voices, *"Salvation belongs to our God, who sits on the throne, and to the Lamb!"* The angels, elders, and the four living creatures join in, falling on their faces and worshiping God, saying, *"Amen! Praise and glory and wisdom and thanks and honor and power and strength be to our God for ever and ever. Amen!"*

This vision is not just an inspiring picture of worship; it reveals important truths about the nature of worship in heaven. First, it is communal and universal, bringing together people from every nation, reflecting the inclusivity of God's kingdom. Worship in heaven transcends cultural and language barriers, pointing to the fact that in heaven, we will worship God as one united body. Second, it is ceaseless. The multitude in this scene are engaged in constant worship, reflecting the truth that in heaven, worship will not be bound by time or fatigue. It will be an eternal act of glorifying the Lord. Lastly, this heavenly worship is marked by humility and reverence, as the angels and elders fall prostrate before God, acknowledging His supreme authority.

Old Testament Example: Isaiah's Vision of Worship

The heavenly model of worship is not limited to the book of Revelation. In **Isaiah 6:1-4,** we find one of the most vivid descriptions of heavenly worship in the Old Testament. Isaiah has a vision of the Lord seated on a throne, high and exalted, with the train of His robe filling the temple. Above Him are the seraphim, angelic beings who are calling to one another, saying, *"Holy, holy, holy is the Lord Almighty; the whole earth is full of His glory."* Their voices are so powerful that the doorposts and thresholds of the temple shake, and the entire space is filled with smoke.

This image of worship in heaven is awe-inspiring. The seraphim are engaged in continuous praise, declaring the holiness of God. The triple repetition of the word *"holy"* emphasizes the complete and utter perfection of God. The shaking of the doorposts and the filling of the temple with smoke are symbolic of God's overwhelming presence. Isaiah's vision reveals that worship in heaven is not just vocal but also deeply experiential. It involves the totality of God's creation responding to His majesty and holiness. This is the worship that we, too, are called to mirror on earth—a worship that is not just about words or rituals but about an encounter with the living God.

New Testament Example: The Worship of Jesus by the Heavenly Host

In the New Testament, the birth of Jesus is another significant moment that is marked by heavenly worship. In **Luke 2:13-14,** after the angel announces the birth of the Savior to the shepherds, *"a multitude of the heavenly host"* appears, praising God and saying, *"Glory to God in the highest, and on earth peace among those with whom He is pleased!"* This scene is often associated with the joyful celebration of Christmas, but it is also a profound example of heavenly worship breaking into the earthly realm.

The heavenly host's worship is spontaneous, joyful, and centered on the person of Jesus Christ. Their praise reflects the immense significance of the Incarnation—the moment when God took on human flesh to dwell among us. In this scene, the angels give glory to God, recognizing that the birth of Jesus is the ultimate expression of His love and plan for salvation. The worship of Jesus by the heavenly host foreshadows the eternal worship that He will receive in heaven, where every knee will bow and every tongue confess that He is Lord (Philippians 2:10-11).

Real-Life Example: Structured vs. Spontaneous Worship

Heavenly worship, as revealed in Scripture, is both structured and spontaneous. On earth, we experience glimpses of this in our own worship practices. Structured liturgical worship, as seen in many traditional churches, reflects the reverence and order of heavenly worship. Liturgies often follow a set pattern, with readings, prayers, hymns, and sacraments that guide worshipers through a journey of reflection and praise. This form of worship can be deeply meaningful, as it helps individuals focus their hearts and minds on God, much like the structured worship we see in Revelation with the multitude and the elders.

On the other hand, spontaneous moments of praise—whether in a personal devotion or a corporate worship setting—also mirror heavenly worship. Just as the angels in Luke 2 suddenly burst into song at the birth of Christ, there are moments in our lives when we are overcome with awe and gratitude for God's goodness. These moments of spontaneous worship can be as simple as singing a hymn while driving, offering a prayer of thanks in a moment of joy, or lifting hands in worship during a church service. Both structured and spontaneous worship are important because they reflect different aspects of the heavenly model of worship. In heaven, worship will be both orderly and overflowing with joy, as we experience the fullness of God's presence.

In real life, these two modes of worship come together to help us grasp the profound nature of worship in heaven. A church service with a well-prepared order of worship can bring us into a posture of reverence, while an unexpected moment of personal praise can remind us of the joy that comes from encountering God's presence. Both are valuable, and both are necessary, as we practice for the eternal worship that awaits us.

Earthly Worship as a Foretaste of Heaven

The heavenly model of worship is one that we are called to imitate on earth. Revelation, Isaiah, and Luke all offer us glimpses of what worship looks like in the presence of God: it is continuous, awe-inspiring, and focused entirely on glorifying the Creator. Whether through structured liturgies or spontaneous outbursts of praise, our worship here on earth is a foretaste of the eternal worship we will experience in heaven.

As we worship, we are not merely performing a religious duty; we are engaging in a divine rehearsal for eternity. The multitudes in heaven, the seraphim in Isaiah's vision, and the heavenly host at Jesus' birth all remind us that worship is our eternal destiny. It is what we were created for. As we lift our voices, our hearts, and our lives in worship, we are joining with the angels, the elders, and the multitude in heaven in proclaiming, *"Holy, holy, holy is the Lord Almighty; the whole earth is full of His glory"* (Isaiah 6:3).

Let our worship on earth be a reflection of the awe, reverence, and joy that fills the courts of heaven. And may we worship with the anticipation that one day, we will join the heavenly throng, standing before the throne of God and the Lamb, proclaiming His glory forever.

The Bride's Readiness – Worship as Preparation

Worship is not merely an expression of reverence or adoration; it is a transformative process that prepares us for our eternal destiny. In the Scriptures, the Church is often described as the bride of Christ, and just as a bride prepares for her wedding day, worship helps us prepare for the ultimate union with Christ at the marriage supper of the Lamb. Through worship, we are cleansed, sanctified, and made ready for the day when we will stand before our Bridegroom. This chapter will explore how worship acts as a vital part of this preparation, using biblical examples and real-life applications to show how worship shapes the heart of the believer.

The Marriage Supper of the Lamb: Revelation 19:7-9

The Apostle John's vision in **Revelation 19:7-9** provides one of the most vivid images of the Church as the bride of Christ. It says, *"Let us rejoice and be glad and give him glory! For the wedding of the Lamb has come, and his bride has made herself ready. Fine linen, bright and clean, was given her to wear."* The fine linen, John explains, stands for "the righteous acts of the saints." This passage reveals the culmination of the Church's journey—standing before Christ, fully prepared, adorned with the righteousness of her worship and works.

In this heavenly scene, worship and preparation are intertwined. The bride, representing the Church, has made herself ready through acts of righteousness, which are the fruit of a life of worship. Worship, then, is not just something we do here and now; it is part of our preparation for an eternal reality. Our worship on earth anticipates this moment of glorious union with Christ, and every act of worship, whether corporate or private, brings us closer to being ready for that great day.

Old Testament Example: Esther's Preparation to Meet the King

A powerful Old Testament example of worship as preparation is found in the story of **Esther**. In **Esther 2:12-17**, we read about Esther's lengthy preparation before meeting King Xerxes. She underwent twelve months of beauty treatments—six months with oil of myrrh and six months with perfumes and cosmetics—before she could be presented to the king. Her time of preparation was essential, and only after this period of careful refinement did she find favor in the eyes of the king.

Esther's preparation is a metaphor for the Church's readiness to meet Christ. Just as Esther was purified and adorned before entering the king's presence, so too must the Church be purified through worship and sanctification before standing before the Lord. Worship helps to cleanse and prepare our hearts. It is in these moments of worship—whether through prayer, song, or meditation on Scripture—that the Holy Spirit works within us, refining us and preparing us for our future in God's eternal kingdom.

New Testament Example: The Parable of the Ten Virgins

In the New Testament, Jesus provides a vivid illustration of preparation for the Bridegroom through the **Parable of the Ten Virgins** in **Matthew 25:1-13**. In this parable, ten virgins take their lamps and go out to meet the bridegroom. Five of them are wise and bring extra oil for their lamps, while the other five are foolish and bring none. When the bridegroom is delayed, all ten fall asleep, but at midnight, the call goes out: *"Here's the bridegroom! Come out to meet him!"* The wise virgins are ready, their lamps filled with oil, but the foolish ones are unprepared and have to go buy more oil. By the time they return, the door to the wedding banquet is shut, and they are left outside.

This parable underscores the necessity of readiness and preparation. The oil in the lamps can be seen as a metaphor for the inner spiritual life, kept alive and burning through worship and intimacy with God. The five wise virgins, who made sure to bring extra oil, represent believers who consistently nourish their relationship with God through worship, prayer, and obedience. In contrast, the foolish virgins symbolize those who neglect their spiritual preparation and are caught unprepared when the time comes to meet the Bridegroom. Worship, in this sense, is the oil that keeps our spiritual lamps burning, ensuring that we are ready when Christ returns.

Real-Life Example: Worship as Personal Preparation

In the life of a believer, personal worship plays a crucial role in spiritual growth and preparation for eternity. Worship is not limited to Sunday services or corporate gatherings; it is a daily practice that shapes our character, refines our hearts, and draws us closer to God. Just as a bride spends time preparing herself for her wedding day, so too must believers spend time in worship, preparing themselves for the ultimate wedding feast with Christ.

Consider the example of a Christian who sets aside time each day for personal worship—whether through singing hymns, reading Scripture, or spending quiet moments in prayer. Over time, this practice begins to shape their character. They grow in patience, love, and humility as they spend more time in God's presence. Their mind is renewed, and their heart is softened. Personal worship acts as a mirror, reflecting the areas of life that need refining and allowing the Holy Spirit to work within them. In this way, worship becomes a form of spiritual preparation, much like Esther's beauty treatments, preparing the believer to stand before the King.

This preparation is not just internal; it has external manifestations as well. A life of worship produces righteous actions—acts of kindness, love, and service—that are the *"fine linen"* we will wear at the marriage supper of the Lamb. Just as the bride in Revelation is adorned with fine linen, bright and clean, representing the righteous acts of the saints, so too do our lives of worship produce fruit that glorifies God and prepares us for our eternal destiny.

Worship as the Bride's Preparation
Worship is an essential part of our spiritual preparation as the bride of Christ. Through worship, we are sanctified, refined, and made ready for the day when we will stand before our Bridegroom. The images of the marriage supper of the Lamb in Revelation, Esther's preparation to meet the king, and the parable of the ten virgins all point to the necessity of readiness. Worship is not just about singing songs or attending church services; it is about cultivating a heart that is prepared to meet the Lord.

As we engage in worship, both corporately and privately, we are participating in a divine process of preparation. Each moment of worship brings us closer to the day when we will join the multitudes in heaven, standing before the throne of God, fully prepared to enter into the joy of our eternal union with Christ. Just as a bride eagerly anticipates her wedding day, so too should we, the Church, anticipate the day when we will be united with our Bridegroom, Jesus Christ. Let our worship be a constant reminder of that great day and a means of preparing our hearts for the eternal wedding feast.

Worship in Spirit and Truth:
A Call for Authenticity

Worship is more than an external expression of devotion; it is the true reflection of our heart's connection with God. In **John 4:24**, Jesus declared, *"God is spirit, and his worshipers must worship in the Spirit and in truth."* This profound statement captures the essence of authentic worship—worship that flows from a sincere heart and is grounded in the truth of who God is. In this chapter, we explore the necessity of worshiping in spirit and truth, drawing from the Old and New Testaments, and considering how genuine worship shapes our spiritual lives and prepares us for eternal communion with God.

Scriptural Foundation: Worship in Spirit and Truth (John 4:24)

Jesus' encounter with the Samaritan woman at the well is one of the most profound teachings on worship found in Scripture. In **John 4:23-24,** Jesus tells her, *"Yet a time is coming and has now come when the true worshipers will worship the Father in the Spirit and in truth, for they are the kind of worshipers the Father seeks. God is spirit, and his worshipers must worship in the Spirit and in truth."*

This teaching emphasizes that true worship is not confined to a particular place or ritual. It transcends physical forms and enters into a deeper realm where the Holy Spirit guides us into the truth of who God is. Worship "in spirit" implies that our hearts are engaged with God, stirred by the Spirit's work within us. Worship *"in truth"* implies that our worship is aligned with the reality of God's nature, character, and promises. Together, worship in spirit and truth reflects the authentic, wholehearted devotion that God desires from His people.

In this encounter, Jesus shifts the focus from the external rituals practiced by the Jews and Samaritans to the internal disposition of the worshiper. He points to a new way of worship, one that is not bound by location (as the Jews worshiped in Jerusalem and the Samaritans on Mount Gerizim) but is instead deeply personal and authentic. This new worship is the kind of worship that prepares us for eternity, where we will stand before God in His full glory, fully aware of His truth.

Old Testament Example: David's Authentic Worship in the Psalms

The Old Testament provides us with a powerful example of authentic worship in the life of King David. Throughout the **Psalms,** David expresses his raw emotions, his fears, his failures, and his triumphs in worship before God. **Psalm 51,** in particular, stands as one of the most heartfelt confessions of sin and a plea for God's mercy. After his sin with Bathsheba, David pours out his heart, saying, *"Create in me a pure heart, O God, and renew a steadfast spirit within me"* (**Psalm 51:10**). This psalm reveals the depth of David's sincerity and his understanding that true worship begins with a contrite heart.

David's life teaches us that authentic worship is not about presenting ourselves as perfect before God; it is about bringing our true selves—our brokenness, our struggles, and our desires—before Him in complete honesty. David's worship in the Psalms shows us that God values authenticity over ritual. He desires worshipers who come to Him with open hearts, willing to be transformed by His grace.

David's example aligns perfectly with the call to worship in spirit and truth, as he constantly sought a deeper, more intimate relationship with God through genuine worship.

New Testament Example: The Woman with the Alabaster Jar

In the New Testament, one of the most profound examples of authentic worship is found in the story of the **woman with the alabaster jar.** In **Luke 7:37-38**, a woman who had lived a sinful life came to Jesus while He was reclining at a Pharisee's table. She brought an alabaster jar of perfume, and as she stood behind Jesus, she began to weep, wetting His feet with her tears and wiping them with her hair. She then poured the expensive perfume on His feet as an act of extravagant love and worship.

This woman's act of worship was deeply personal and sincere. Despite the judgment of those around her, she worshiped Jesus with complete abandonment, offering all she had in gratitude and love. Her worship was not about following a prescribed form or ritual; it was a spontaneous expression of her heart, rooted in the truth of who Jesus was. She knew she was in the presence of the Messiah, the one who could forgive her sins and redeem her life. Her act of worship was an embodiment of worship in spirit and truth.

Jesus honored her worship, telling her, *"Your sins are forgiven"* (**Luke 7:48**), and commending her faith. This story illustrates that authentic worship is not about impressing others or following cultural norms. It is about coming to Jesus with a heart full of love, humility, and truth. This woman's worship reflects the kind of worship that will take place in heaven, where all barriers are removed, and the only response is pure adoration of the Lamb.

Real-Life Example: The Transformative Power of Genuine Worship

In our daily lives, genuine worship has the power to transform us in profound ways. When we come before God in true worship—engaging our hearts and minds fully, seeking His presence, and acknowledging His truth—something shifts within us. Our priorities realign, our burdens become lighter, and our spirits are renewed.

Consider the experience of a believer who, during a difficult season, turns to God in worship despite feeling weighed down by anxiety or sorrow. As they lift their voice in song, even in the privacy of their own home, they begin to sense God's presence in a powerful way. Their tears may flow, much like the woman with the alabaster jar, but through those moments of worship, their heart is softened, and their faith is strengthened. This kind of worship brings about real spiritual change because it is authentic—it comes from a place of truth, where the worshiper is not hiding their pain but bringing it before God.

Many people have shared testimonies of how worship has been a source of healing and transformation in their lives. Whether it is through singing hymns, engaging in communal worship at church, or spending quiet moments in personal prayer, the act of worship can be a gateway to deeper intimacy with God. It is in these moments of sincere worship that we catch a glimpse of what heaven will be like—a place where worship is continuous, pure, and unhindered by the distractions of this world.

The Call for Authentic Worship
Worship in spirit and truth is more than just an instruction from Jesus—it is an invitation to enter into a deeper, more genuine relationship with God. The examples of David's heartfelt worship in the Psalms, the woman with the alabaster jar, and countless real-life experiences show us that God desires worship that flows from the heart. When we worship in spirit, we are allowing the Holy Spirit to guide us into a place of genuine connection with God. When we worship in truth, we acknowledge who God is—His majesty, holiness, and love—and respond accordingly.

Authentic worship prepares us for the eternal worship we will one day experience in heaven. Just as the Samaritan woman learned from Jesus that true worship is not bound by external rituals but is about the heart's connection to God, so too must we embrace this call to worship in spirit and truth. This is the worship that will prepare us for the day when we stand before the throne of God, joining the multitudes in heaven who worship Him forever. Let our earthly worship be a rehearsal for that heavenly reality, a reflection of our love and devotion to the One who is worthy of all praise.

Corporate Worship – A Picture of Unity in Heaven

Corporate worship, where believers gather to glorify God together, offers a powerful glimpse of the unity that will one day characterize heaven. Throughout Scripture, worship is often depicted as a communal experience, where diverse people come together in a shared expression of reverence for God. In **Revelation 7:9**, we see this fully realized in heaven, where *"a great multitude that no one could count, from every nation, tribe, people, and language"* stands before the throne and worships God as one. This heavenly picture of unity is the ultimate destination for corporate worship on earth, where believers of every background join to reflect God's eternal kingdom.

Worship and Unity in Heaven (Revelation 7:9-12)

The book of Revelation gives us a powerful vision of worship in heaven. In **Revelation 7:9-12**, the apostle John describes an awe-inspiring scene where a great multitude of people, too numerous to count, stand before the throne of God and the Lamb. These worshipers come from *"every nation, tribe, people, and language,"* symbolizing the unity and diversity of God's people. In unison, they cry out: *"Salvation belongs to our God, who sits on the throne, and to the Lamb."*

This heavenly scene is a reflection of God's ultimate plan for humanity—to unite people from every background, culture, and nation in the worship of Him. The diversity of the multitude in heaven is a testament to the universal reach of the gospel and the unifying power of worship. No longer divided by earthly distinctions, the worshipers are united in their common adoration of God. This vision sets the standard for what corporate worship on earth should strive for—a foretaste of the perfect unity and harmony that awaits us in heaven.

In this heavenly picture, we see that worship is not an isolated or individual act but one that brings people together. Corporate worship on earth, when done in the spirit of unity, reflects this heavenly reality. It is in these moments of shared worship that we experience a glimpse of what is to come—the joy of standing together as one body before God, praising Him with hearts and voices united.

Old Testament Example: Solomon's Dedication of the Temple (2 Chronicles 5:13-14)

The dedication of Solomon's temple provides one of the most powerful examples of unified worship in the Old Testament. In **2 Chronicles 5:13-14**, as the ark of the covenant is brought into the temple, we read that the musicians and singers joined together in unison to praise the Lord. They sang, *"He is good; His love endures forever,"* and the cloud of God's glory filled the temple, so much so that the priests could not continue their duties.

This event signifies the profound connection between unity in worship and the manifest presence of God. When the people of Israel worshiped together with one heart and one voice, God's presence descended upon them in a tangible way. The unified worship of the people created an atmosphere where God's glory could be revealed, and this unity in worship is a foretaste of the worship that will occur in heaven, where all believers will come together as one to experience the fullness of God's presence.

The significance of this moment lies in the collective participation of the people. It was not just the priests or the Levites who worshiped, but all of Israel was involved. This corporate expression of worship became a powerful demonstration of their devotion to God and their shared identity as His people. Just as Solomon's temple dedication brought the people together, worship today serves as a unifying force for believers, transcending differences and bringing us into a shared encounter with God.

New Testament Example: The Early Church Worshiping Together (Acts 2:42-47)

In the New Testament, the early church provides a model for corporate worship that is grounded in unity and fellowship. **Acts 2:42-47** gives us a glimpse into the worship practices of the first Christians, describing how they *"devoted themselves to the apostles' teaching and to fellowship, to the breaking of bread and to prayer."* The believers met together daily in the temple courts and in their homes, praising God with glad and sincere hearts.

This passage highlights the communal aspect of worship in the early church. Their worship was not limited to formal gatherings, but it permeated their everyday lives. The believers were united in their devotion to God and to one another, and their worship flowed naturally out of their shared life in Christ. Their unity in worship was a reflection of the unity they experienced as the body of Christ.

What is particularly striking about the early church is the diversity of people who came together in worship. Acts 2 records that on the day of Pentecost, people from every nation under heaven were gathered in Jerusalem, and the Holy Spirit empowered the apostles to speak in different languages so that everyone could hear the gospel in their own tongue. This miraculous event marked the beginning of a new era of worship—one that transcended cultural and linguistic barriers. The unity of the early church in worship was a direct result of the work of the Holy Spirit, who brings believers from all backgrounds into one body.

The early church's corporate worship serves as a model for the church today. It reminds us that worship is not just a personal experience but a communal one. As believers, we are called to come together in worship, united by our shared faith in Christ. When we gather to worship, we participate in a heavenly reality where all of God's people, from every nation and generation, will worship Him together in perfect unity.

Real-Life Example: The Global Church's Worship Practices Today

In our world today, the global church reflects the diversity and unity that will one day characterize worship in heaven. From mega-churches in the United States to small house churches in China, from exuberant African praise services to quiet, contemplative worship in European cathedrals, believers from every corner of the earth are joining together in worship. These diverse expressions of worship are a powerful testimony to the universal nature of the gospel and the unifying power of Christ.

Consider a global worship event, such as the **Global Day of Prayer**, where millions of Christians from around the world come together to worship and pray in unity. In these moments, geographical, cultural, and denominational barriers fade away, and the focus is entirely on God. These gatherings are a foretaste of the heavenly worship described in

Revelation, where believers from every nation will stand together before God, praising Him as one.

In many churches, the music, language, and style of worship may vary, but the heart of worship remains the same—exalting God as Lord and Savior. Whether through the singing of hymns, the raising of hands in praise, or the quiet reflection of prayer, corporate worship unites us as the body of Christ. It allows us to experience, in part, the unity that we will one day fully know in heaven.

Corporate Worship as a Foretaste of Heaven

Corporate worship is more than just a gathering of individuals—it is a powerful picture of the unity that will characterize heaven. As we come together to worship, we join in a shared expression of praise that transcends our individual differences and reflects the heavenly reality where people from every nation will worship God together as one.

Through the examples of Solomon's temple dedication and the early church, we see that corporate worship has always been a vital part of God's plan for His people. It is in these moments of unified worship that we encounter God's presence in a unique and powerful way. Just as the cloud of God's glory filled the temple when the people of Israel worshiped together, so too does God's presence fill our worship when we gather as one body in Christ.

As we look to the future, we are reminded that our corporate worship on earth is a rehearsal for the eternal worship that will take place in heaven. When we gather to worship, we are participating in a foretaste of the unity, diversity, and glory that will define our eternal experience with God. Let us, therefore, approach corporate worship with a heart of unity, knowing that in these moments, we are preparing for the day when we will stand before God with believers from every nation, tribe, people, and language, worshiping Him forever.

The Joy of Worship – A Foretaste of Eternal Bliss

Worship is not merely a duty but a profound delight that opens the heart to experience the joy of God's presence. Throughout the Bible, worship is consistently linked to joy, celebration, and the deep satisfaction of being in communion with the Creator. This chapter explores how earthly worship provides a foretaste of the overwhelming joy and fulfillment we will experience in heaven, where we will worship God in His fullness forever.

Joy in Worship: A Glimpse of Heaven

Worship on earth allows us to experience, in part, the joy that awaits us in heaven. In the Scriptures, joy is often associated with being in the presence of God. **Psalm 16:11** beautifully captures this: *"You make known to me the path of life; in Your presence, there is fullness of joy; at Your right hand are pleasures forevermore."* This verse paints a vivid picture of the joy that comes from communion with God. The joy found in worship is not a fleeting, surface-level emotion but a deep, abiding sense of fulfillment and satisfaction that comes from being near the One who created and loves us.

The joy of worship is a foretaste of what we will experience in eternity. In heaven, we will stand before God, fully aware of His majesty and love, and our worship will be pure and uninhibited. The joy that we experience now in moments of true worship is a reflection, albeit incomplete, of the eternal bliss that awaits us. In these moments, we catch a glimpse of the heavenly worship that will be our eternal reality.

Old Testament Example: The Joyous Celebration of the Ark's Return (2 Samuel 6:14-15)

In the Old Testament, one of the most vivid examples of joy in worship is found in the story of King David celebrating the return of the Ark of the Covenant to Jerusalem. The Ark represented the presence of God among His people, and its return was a moment of great spiritual significance and joy for Israel. **2 Samuel 6:14-15** describes how David "danced before the Lord with all his might" as he led the procession, and the people of Israel shouted with joy and the sound of trumpets filled the air.

David's uninhibited expression of worship demonstrates the kind of joy that arises when God's presence is near. His dance before the Lord was an outward manifestation of the joy and gratitude he felt in his heart. The entire nation celebrated as the Ark, the symbol of God's covenant with His people, was brought into the city.

This moment also prefigures the joy of eternal worship in heaven. Just as David and the people rejoiced in God's presence, we too will experience unspeakable joy when we stand before God in eternity. The joy of that day will far surpass anything we can imagine, but David's celebration gives us a glimpse of the kind of joy we can look forward to in heaven—a joy that flows from being in the presence of God and participating in His redemptive work.

New Testament Example: The Apostles' Joy After Receiving the Holy Spirit (Acts 2:46-47)

In the New Testament, the early church offers another powerful example of the joy that comes from worship. After the outpouring of the Holy Spirit at Pentecost, the apostles and early believers experienced a profound sense of joy and unity. **Acts**

2:46-47 describes how they *"continued daily with one accord in the temple, and breaking bread from house to house, they ate their food with gladness and simplicity of heart, praising God and having favor with all the people."*

The joy that filled the early church was the result of their encounter with the Holy Spirit and their shared worship of God. Their worship was not confined to a single day or place; it permeated their daily lives, and their joy was evident in their fellowship, generosity, and praise. The early believers understood that worship was not merely a ritual but a way of life—a continuous act of devotion that filled them with gladness and a deep sense of spiritual fulfillment.

This joy reflects the work of the Holy Spirit, who empowers and inspires worship. As believers, when we gather to worship, we are not just going through the motions but are engaging with the Holy Spirit, who brings life, joy, and transformation to our worship. The apostles' experience reminds us that worship is a source of deep joy, not just in this life but as a foretaste of the eternal joy we will experience in God's presence.

Real-Life Example: Personal Experiences of Joy in Worship

Many believers can testify to moments of deep joy and fulfillment during worship. Whether in a communal gathering or in personal prayer, worship often brings with it an overwhelming sense of peace and joy that transcends circumstances. There are countless testimonies of individuals who have encountered God in powerful ways during worship, and these experiences have brought them a profound sense of joy and spiritual renewal.

For example, consider the story of a believer who, during a worship service, felt a sudden and powerful awareness of God's love and presence. In that moment, the weight of their burdens lifted, and they were filled with an indescribable joy. They knew they were not just singing songs but were encountering the living God, and this experience brought them a deep and lasting sense of peace and contentment.

Such experiences remind us that worship is not just about songs or rituals but about encountering God and being transformed by His presence. The joy that comes from these moments of worship is a taste of the eternal joy we will experience in heaven, where we will be in God's presence forever, worshiping Him with unending joy and fulfillment.

Worship as a Foretaste of Eternal Joy
Worship on earth is a profound and joyous experience, but it is only a glimpse of the eternal joy that awaits us in heaven. In worship, we encounter the presence of God, and in His presence, there is fullness of joy (Psalm 16:11). From the joyous celebration of David at the return of the Ark of the Covenant to the early church's spirit-filled worship, Scripture is filled with examples of how worship brings joy to the hearts of God's people.

As believers, we are invited to experience this joy in worship here on earth, knowing that it is a foretaste of the eternal joy that will be ours in heaven. When we gather to worship, whether in large assemblies or in quiet personal moments, we are participating in a divine reality that points us toward our ultimate destiny—worshiping God in His presence for all eternity. The joy we experience in worship now is a precious gift, one that prepares us for the eternal joy we will have in heaven, where we will worship God with fullness of heart and soul, forever and ever.

The Eternal Feast – Worship in the New Creation

Worship in its fullest expression is the eternal communion between God and His people, a feast that will last forever in the new creation. This chapter delves into how the Bible frames the culmination of worship as an eternal celebration with God. In both the Old and New Testaments, feasts play a central role in God's relationship with His people, and these earthly celebrations point to a greater, eternal feast that will take place in heaven. Our anticipation of this heavenly banquet shapes our worship today, reminding us that our worship is not confined to earthly gatherings but is part of the eternal narrative of redemption.

Worship as Eternal Communion

The Bible paints a vivid picture of worship in heaven as an eternal communion with God, where His presence will be with His people forever. **Revelation 21:3** declares: *"And I heard a loud voice from the throne saying, 'Look! God's dwelling place is now among the people, and He will dwell with them. They will be His people, and God Himself will be with them and be their God.'"* This verse speaks of the culmination of God's desire to dwell with humanity. No longer separated by sin or the limitations of the physical world, worship in heaven will be a complete, unbroken relationship between God and His people.

This eternal communion is often described as a feast, where the joy of fellowship and worship reaches its fullest form. In heaven, we will be part of an eternal banquet, celebrating with God and all His people across every nation and time. **Revelation**

19:9 describes this ultimate celebration: "Blessed are those who are invited to the marriage supper of the Lamb." This heavenly feast is the culmination of the redemptive story, where all of God's people, past and present, come together in perfect harmony to worship Him in glory.

Old Testament Example: The Passover as a Foretaste of the Heavenly Feast

The Passover in the Old Testament is one of the most profound examples of how an earthly feast prefigures the eternal feast in heaven. Instituted in **Exodus 12**, the Passover was a commemorative feast to remind the Israelites of God's deliverance from slavery in Egypt. It involved the sacrifice of a lamb, whose blood was placed on the doorposts of each Israelite home, symbolizing the covering and protection of God's people. Every year, the Israelites celebrated this feast as a remembrance of their freedom and covenant with God.

Yet, the Passover was more than just a historical event. It pointed forward to an even greater deliverance and celebration. Just as the Israelites were delivered from physical slavery, humanity would one day be delivered from the slavery of sin through the ultimate Passover Lamb—Jesus Christ. The Passover feast is a shadow of the eternal feast we will enjoy in heaven. In heaven, we will celebrate the fullness of our deliverance from sin, death, and separation from God. As the Israelites rejoiced in their earthly redemption, we will rejoice in our eternal redemption.

New Testament Example: The Lord's Supper as a Foretaste of the Heavenly Banquet

The New Testament provides a clear connection between earthly worship and the heavenly feast through the institution of the Lord's Supper. On the night before His crucifixion, Jesus shared the Passover meal with His disciples, but He transformed it into something new. **Matthew 26:29** records Jesus' words: *"I tell you, I will not drink from this fruit of the vine from now on until that day when I drink it new with you in My Father's kingdom."* In this statement, Jesus connected the act of communion with the future celebration in the Kingdom of God.

The Lord's Supper, also known as Communion, is an act of remembrance for Christians, celebrating Christ's sacrificial death and resurrection. However, it is also a foretaste of the heavenly banquet to come. Each time we partake of the bread and wine, we are reminded that we will one day join Christ at the eternal feast, where we will be in His presence forever. Communion points beyond the present moment and directs our hearts toward the future, where the joy of salvation will be fully realized in the new creation.

Real-Life Example: The Church's Celebration of Communion

In modern worship, the act of Communion serves as a powerful reminder of the heavenly feast we anticipate. Churches around the world regularly practice this sacrament, reflecting on Jesus' sacrifice and the hope of His return. When believers gather to partake in Communion, they are not just remembering an event from the past; they are actively participating in a spiritual reality that points forward to eternity.

Consider the experience of a believer who, during Communion, is struck by the weight of Christ's love and sacrifice. As they take the bread and wine, they feel a deep connection not only to the historical event of the cross but also to the future promise of eternal life with God. This sacred moment becomes a glimpse of the eternal feast, where all of God's people will gather in celebration of His goodness and grace.

Communion, in this way, is both a reflection of the past and a foretaste of the future. It ties believers to the ancient tradition of the Passover and to the future reality of the marriage supper of the Lamb. Each time we gather for this sacrament, we are reminded that our worship on earth is leading us toward an eternal worship experience with God, where joy and fellowship will know no bounds.

Worship as Preparation for the Eternal Feast

Worship on earth is a preparation for the eternal feast that awaits us in heaven. As we gather in churches, homes, and communities to celebrate Communion, sing praises, and offer prayers, we are participating in a heavenly reality that will one day be fully realized. Just as the Passover pointed forward to Christ's redemptive work and the Lord's Supper points forward to the marriage supper of the Lamb, our earthly worship is a rehearsal for the eternal celebration that will take place in the new creation.

In that day, God's dwelling place will be with His people, and we will feast together in perfect unity and joy. All of the brokenness, pain, and sorrow of this world will be wiped away, and we will stand in the glorious presence of God, worshiping Him in spirit and truth for all eternity. Worship today, whether through songs of praise, acts of service, or the sharing of Communion, is an invitation to participate in the eternal story of God's redemptive plan. As we worship, we are reminded that the best is yet to come—the eternal feast where we will be united with God and all His people in perfect love and joy forever.

Daily Master Plan for Becoming a True Worshipper: A Step-by-Step Approach

True worship isn't just a ritual; it's the complete involvement of our body, soul, and spirit as we respond to the presence of God. As we seek to worship God in spirit and truth (John 4:23-24), this daily master plan is designed to help you align every part of your being—your breath, heart, hands, and head—with God's will, using Scripture as your guide. This plan will help you view worship not as a task but as a natural outflow of who you are in Christ, honoring God with every breath you take.

1. Start the Day with Breath Awareness (Acknowledge God's Life in You)

- ✓ Key Scripture: **Genesis 2:7** – *"Then the LORD God formed man of the dust from the ground, and breathed into his nostrils the breath of life; and man became a living being."*
- ✓ **Morning Action:** As soon as you wake up, before your feet touch the ground, pause and take a deep breath. Reflect on the fact that God's breath is in you. Each breath you take is a reminder of His life-giving power. Acknowledge that your very existence is a result of His grace.
- ✓ **Prayer**: *"Lord, thank You for breathing Your life into me. Help me to use every breath today to glorify You."*
- ✓ **Example**: Practice breathing deeply and mindfully throughout the day, using each breath to re-center your focus on God. Just as

breath sustains life, so does God's presence sustain your spirit.
- ✓ **How this helps worship**: Being conscious of your breath helps you maintain an attitude of gratitude and worship, acknowledging God's continual sustenance in your life.

2. Engage Your Heart (Surrender Your Will and Emotions to God)

- ✓ Key Scripture: **Proverbs 4:23** – *"Above all else, guard your heart, for everything you do flows from it."*
- ✓ **Morning Devotion**: After breathing, take time to surrender your heart to God. Your heart represents your emotions, desires, and will. Read a passage from the Psalms, such as **Psalm 51**, where David pours out his heart in worship and surrender.
- ✓ **Action**: Write down or reflect on your emotions, desires, and struggles. Surrender them to God in prayer, asking Him to align your heart with His will. Ask for the fruit of the Spirit (Galatians 5:22-23) to govern your emotions throughout the day.
- ✓ **Example**: Reflect on David's heart for worship. In **2 Samuel 6:14**, David danced before the Lord with all his might. His heart was wholly focused on the joy of God's presence. Worship God from the heart, knowing that authenticity is what God desires.
- ✓ **How this helps worship**: Surrendering your heart allows your emotions and desires to be purified, so your worship becomes more genuine and heartfelt, not just a performance or routine.

3. Use Your Hands (Commit to Acts of Service as Worship)

- ✓ Key Scripture: **Colossians 3:23** – *"Whatever you do, work at it with all your heart, as working for the Lord, not for human masters."*
- ✓ **Daily Activity**: As you go about your day, use your hands for acts of service and kindness. Worship is not confined to singing or prayer but extends to how we live and serve others.
- ✓ **Action**: Consciously dedicate your tasks—whether at work, home, or elsewhere—to God. For instance, when washing dishes, caring for children, or working on a project, remember that these small actions can be worship when done for God's glory.
- ✓ **Example**: Jesus Himself demonstrated this in **John 13:1-17** when He washed His disciples' feet. By humbly serving others, you reflect Christ's love and elevate your daily work into an act of worship.
- ✓ **How this helps worship**: By involving your hands in acts of service, you worship God through obedience and humility, honoring Him in practical ways.

4. Align Your Head (Renew Your Mind in God's Word)

- ✓ Key Scripture: **Romans 12:2** – *"Do not conform to the pattern of this world, but be transformed by the renewing of your mind."*
- ✓ **Midday Meditation**: Set aside time during the day to renew your mind by meditating on Scripture. Read a passage that reminds you of God's character, such as **Isaiah 40**, which speaks of God's greatness and sovereignty.

✓ **Action**: Meditate on the Word. Allow it to transform your thoughts and decisions. Instead of reacting to situations out of habit, filter your thoughts through the lens of Scripture. Pray over challenging passages and seek God's guidance in understanding His will.

✓ **Example**: Jesus, in **Matthew 4:1-11**, used Scripture to combat temptation. By constantly renewing your mind with God's Word, your worship becomes deeper, rooted in truth rather than emotions or traditions.

✓ **How this helps worship**: When your mind is aligned with Scripture, your thoughts and actions reflect God's truth, making your worship more sincere and grounded in His Word.

5. Engage in Collective Worship (Join Others in Worship)

✓ Key Scripture: **Hebrews 10:25** – *"Not giving up meeting together, as some are in the habit of doing, but encouraging one another—and all the more as you see the Day approaching."*

✓ **Evening Reflection**: End your day by reflecting on your personal worship and how you can engage with others in worship. Whether through corporate prayer, Bible study, or a small gathering, community worship is a vital part of a true worshipper's life.

✓ **Action**: If possible, join others for evening prayer or worship. If alone, reflect on the unity of the body of Christ. Pray for your local church and global believers, lifting them up to God in unity.

- ✓ **Example**: The early church in **Acts 2:42-47** devoted themselves to fellowship and worship. Even if you can't meet in person, engaging in prayer for others unites your heart with the global body of believers.
- ✓ **How this helps worship**: Corporate worship reminds you that worship isn't just individual but communal, as God desires unity in His body. Joining others in worship allows you to experience the fullness of God's presence.

6. Surrender in Rest (Worship Through Trust and Rest)

- ✓ Key Scripture: **Psalm 4:8** – *"In peace I will lie down and sleep, for You alone, LORD, make me dwell in safety."*
- ✓ **Night Prayer**: Before you sleep, take time to surrender your day to God. Rest is an act of trust, acknowledging that even while you sleep, God is at work. Worship doesn't end when your day ends; it continues as you trust in His sovereignty.
- ✓ **Action**: Pray for peace and rest, surrendering any anxieties or unfinished tasks to God. As you lay down, reflect on **Matthew 11:28**, where Jesus invites us to rest in Him. Trust that your rest is an act of worship, showing reliance on God.
- ✓ **Example**: Jesus Himself modeled the importance of rest, often withdrawing to lonely places to pray (Luke 5:16). Resting in God's presence is not inactivity but worship in trust.
- ✓ **How this helps worship**: Surrendering in rest is an acknowledgment that God is sovereign. When you lay down your cares, you offer your

worries and life to Him, making even your sleep an act of worship.

Worship as a Lifestyle

Becoming a true worshipper is about more than singing or attending church—it's about aligning every aspect of your life with God's presence. From the breath in your lungs to the works of your hands, from the thoughts in your head to the emotions in your heart, worship involves every part of who you are. Through daily actions and reflections grounded in Scripture, your entire being can become a living sacrifice, holy and pleasing to God (Romans 12:1). Let your worship be as constant as your breath, as joyful as your service, and as transformative as your mind renewed in Christ.

A Worship Song, Centered around Praising and Magnifying JESUS

Verse 1
Jesus, You are my King and Light,
Your love shines through the darkest night.
In You, my soul finds endless grace,
Your mercy fills each sacred space.

Verse 2
You reign in power, high above,
Your name declares eternal love.
No other name can save or heal,
In You alone, our hearts are sealed.

Verse 3
Majestic Savior, full of might,
Your presence makes the darkness bright.
The angels bow before Your throne,
I lift my praise to You alone.

Verse 4
In every storm, You are my peace,
Your voice commands the waves to cease.
My worship rises like the dawn,
For You, my King, I sing this song.

Verse 5
No other name is higher still,
In You, O Lord, my heart is filled.
I lay my life before Your feet,
In You alone, I am complete.

Verse 6

Forever, Jesus, You will reign,
Your glory never fades or wanes.
I lift my hands, my voice, my soul,
In worship, You alone are whole.

Conclusion:
Worship Now, Worship Forever

Worship is not limited to time and space; it transcends earthly realms and is a glimpse of what will happen eternally. The act of worship here on earth prepares believers for the ultimate reality of being in God's presence forever, where worship will not cease but continue in perfect unity and joy. This chapter explores how our current acts of worship are merely rehearsals for the worship we will offer in eternity and how this shapes both our earthly lives and our eternal perspective.

The Eternal Nature of Worship: Worship Now, Worship Forever

In **Philippians 2:10-11**, the apostle Paul paints a vivid picture of the future of worship: *"At the name of Jesus, every knee should bow, in heaven and on earth and under the earth, and every tongue confess that Jesus Christ is Lord, to the glory of God the Father."* This verse reveals that worship is not merely a temporary act but an eternal one. All of creation will one day bow in worship before the Lordship of Christ, and our earthly worship serves as a precursor to this cosmic event.

On earth, worship is often imperfect due to human distractions, limitations, and sin, but in heaven, worship will be complete and perfect. Every knee bowing signifies full surrender, and every tongue confessing points to the verbal acknowledgment of Jesus' authority. As believers, our current worship anticipates this future reality, reminding us that our ultimate purpose is to glorify God forever. In light of this, every moment of earthly worship should be viewed not as an obligation but as a foretaste of the worship to come.

Living a Life of Worship on Earth: Citizens of Heaven

Scripture reminds us that although we live on earth, our true citizenship is in heaven. **Philippians 3:20** says, *"But our citizenship is in heaven, and we eagerly await a Savior from there, the Lord Jesus Christ."* Our daily lives are an opportunity to reflect this heavenly citizenship by worshiping God through our actions, words, and thoughts. Worship, in this sense, is not limited to a church setting or a Sunday service but is woven into every aspect of life.

In the Old Testament, King David modeled a life of worship that extended beyond ritual. **Psalm 145** is a beautiful reflection of David's worship, where he proclaims, *"I will exalt you, my God the King; I will praise your name for ever and ever."* David's life shows us that worship is both an intentional act of adoration and a way of living that honors God in every situation.

The New Testament church, as described in **Acts 2:46-47**, offers another example of what it means to live a life of worship. The early believers devoted themselves to teaching, fellowship, breaking bread, and prayer. These activities were acts of worship that glorified God and built the community of faith. Their lives became living testimonies of God's grace and power, and their joy in worship was contagious, drawing others to Christ. Worship, for them, was not confined to a singular place but was present in their daily interactions and service to one another.

Real-Life Example: Worship Shapes Our Eternal Perspective

Living a life of worship changes how we see the world and ourselves. When we adopt the mindset of worship, we begin to view every part of life through an eternal lens. The apostle Paul wrote in **Colossians 3:1-2**, *"Set your hearts on things above, where Christ is, seated at the right hand of God. Set your minds on things above, not on earthly things."* This scripture challenges believers to focus on the eternal rather than the temporary, recognizing that everything we do on earth points to the greater reality of heaven.

Consider the life of a modern-day worshipper who understands that their time on earth is a preparation for eternity. This person doesn't simply view worship as singing on Sunday but sees their daily interactions—whether at work, home, or school—as opportunities to glorify God. By helping a colleague, loving a neighbor, or caring for a family member, they are living out their worship. This individual knows that worship is not about escaping the world but about transforming it, offering every moment as a sacrifice of praise (Romans 12:1).

For instance, a believer who spends time in both private and corporate worship is consciously preparing their heart for heaven. In their personal life, they may start their day with gratitude, praising God for His goodness, and end their day in prayer, thanking Him for the blessings received. At church, they gather with fellow believers, knowing that this gathering is a small reflection of the heavenly assembly where all nations, tribes, and tongues will worship together before the throne of God

(Revelation 7:9). Through these acts, their earthly worship cultivates a mindset focused on eternity.

Anticipating the Final Worship in Heaven

The Bible provides us with beautiful glimpses of what worship will look like in the new creation. **Revelation 21:3** says, *"Look! God's dwelling place is now among the people, and he will dwell with them. They will be his people, and God himself will be with them and be their God."* This passage speaks of the culmination of history, where God and His people will dwell together in perfect unity, and worship will be the eternal occupation of the saints.

Imagine the most awe-inspiring worship service you've ever experienced on earth—the collective singing, the heartfelt prayers, the palpable presence of God. Now magnify that infinitely. That is what awaits us in heaven. There will be no more distractions, no more sin, and no more separation from God. The heavenly worship service will be filled with unending joy, peace, and communion with our Creator.

The eternal feast described in **Revelation 19:6-9**, where the saints are invited to the *"marriage supper of the Lamb,"* is another vivid picture of worship in heaven. This feast is not just a meal but a celebration of Christ's victory and the church's eternal union with Him. Our earthly celebrations of communion, where we remember Christ's sacrifice, point to this heavenly banquet, where we will worship Jesus face to face.

Worship Is Our Eternal Calling

Worship is the one thing we do on earth that will continue in heaven. Every act of worship we engage in now is practice for the day when we will join the heavenly chorus and worship God forever. As

Philippians 2:10-11 promises, every knee will bow, and every tongue will confess that Jesus is Lord. Whether through song, service, prayer, or daily obedience, we are preparing for that moment when worship will be our eternal occupation.

By living a life of worship now, we are already participating in the eternal reality of God's kingdom. Each time we worship, we are reminded that we are citizens of heaven, called to reflect His glory in everything we do. Worship, then, is not just what we do—it is who we are. We are worshippers, created to glorify God both now and forever.

In the words of **Psalm 150:6**, *"Let everything that has breath praise the Lord."* As long as we have breath in our lungs, we are called to worship. And one day, when we stand before the throne of God, our worship will be perfected as we join the multitude of saints and angels in praising Him for all eternity. Worship now, and worship forever.

About the Author
'GERARD ASSEY'

Gerard Assey is a Graduate in Economics, a PGD in Management (HRD) and holds a Doctorate in Leadership. Gerard holds several International Qualifications in Sales, Debt Collection, Training & Teaching, and is a 'Fellow' of the prestigious 'Institute of Sales & Marketing Management'-UK, a Certified NLP Practitioner, a 'Certified Trainer', an 'Accredited Management Teacher-Behavioral Sciences', a 'Certified Competency Facilitator', a 'Certified Management Consultant'- (the International credentials of a professional management consultant, awarded in accordance with global standards of the ICMCI); and a Certification from the University of Michigan in 'Successful Negotiation: Essential Strategies and Skills'

He is also a Member of the 'National Association of Sales Professionals' backed with several years experience in varied industries, both in India and Overseas. He also holds an 'Etiquette Consultant' Certification from the USA (by Sue Fox, Author of Best Seller: 'Business Etiquette for Dummies'. She has trained some of the top celebrities' world over). He was also a recipient of a scholarship for extensive training in Japan on 'Corporate Management for India'.

Gerard Assey is 'Founder & Chief Corporate Trainer' of the Group: **'Citius, Altius, Fortius Unlimited'**- an organization that **celebrated 20 years of Glorious Service** in 2021, focusing on 3 Core Competencies:

People. Performance. Profit; in functional areas of Sales & Marketing, HR & Organizational Development, covering Recruitment, Training & Consultancy!

Having managed organizations with large Sales Forces in India & Overseas, his specialization cover extensive areas of Sales Training (All levels - Presentation, Negotiation, Key/ Strategic Accounts Management & Managerial Skills for all sectors), Bid Proposal/ Capture Planning/ Management Trainings, Retail Sales, Customer Service & Customer Retention Programs, Training for Prevention & Collection of Debt, Self & Personal Development Programs (Time Management, Teamwork & Team Building, Business Etiquette & Personal Grooming, Leadership & Managerial Skills, People Management Skills, Train-the-Trainer etc), including preparation of Custom-designed Business Manuals for Internal (HR, Induction, and Sales etc) & External use (Instruction, User Manuals).

Gerard has successfully conducted over 6200 Trainings & Workshops (as of June '24) all across India, Middle East, Africa, Europe & S.E. Asia. Besides public programs conducted regularly, both in India & Overseas, he has some of the top names as clients whom he services from Single Owners to large Public & Government undertakings, covering all sectors, for their in-house needs.

His website: www.CollectionSkills.com is the only one in this part of the world to be featured in the 'Collections & Credit Risk Magazine-USA' under 'Who's Who in Training' and ranks TOP, along with other websites listed below on most search engines.

Gerard is author of 152 books already (Oct 2024), all the books being available on all online platforms and outlets as E-books and Paperbacks

A few of our business related books:

1. Bite-sized Bits on Commonsense Management
2. Heart to Heart on Life's Principles'
3. How to become a Successful Manager
4. The Sales Professionals' Master Workbook of S.Y.S.T.E.M.S
5. The Professional Business Email Etiquette Handbook & Guide
6. The Professional Business Video-Conferencing Etiquette Handbook & Guide
7. Professional Presentation Skills
8. Exceptional Customer Service
9. Professional Tele-Marketing Skills
10. Professional Debt Collection Skills
11. The G.R.E.A.T. Sales & Service Workbook
12. Sales Training Advantage for Results (*The Ultimate Sales Training Manual to enable you stand out as a S.T.A.R.*)
13. CEO Daily Planner & Organizer
14. The Sales Professionals' Master Daily Planner
15. The Professional Debt Collector's Master Daily Planner
16. My Daily Planner & Organizer
17. MY EMERGENCY INFORMATION RECORD (Family Emergency & Peace of Mind Planner)
18. The Ultimate Therapist & Counselors Planner and Organizer
19. Building an Ethical Workplace
20. Managing Relationships at Work
21. Managing Business Meetings Effectively
22. Effective Delegation Skills
23. Goal Setting for Success
24. B2B Selling by Email
25. Professional Business Etiquette & Grooming
26. Dining Etiquette & Table Manners
27. Effective Networking Skills
28. Grooming, Etiquette & Manners for Teens, Young Adults & Future Leaders
29. Inter-Personal Skills
30. Get Ready, Get Hired!
31. Selling in a Recession

From the Ministry side, Gerard graduated in the very first batch of Charis Bible College-India & had for over 9 years served as a Part-time Faculty at Charis Bible College-Chennai (Andrew Wommack Ministries-Colorado, USA).

He is also a graduate of the Advanced Mentorship Program (AMP) and the Circle Of Ministerial Engagement (C.O.M.E.) of Prophet Jerome Fernando and a Spiritual Son of the Esteemed Prophet.

An accomplished author of several Secular & Christian Books, Gerard has been on the board of a few international organizations and boasts of being the SON of the MOST HIGH GOD: An ordinary guy following an extraordinary GOD!

…And some of his most recent Christian Books being:
1. A Bouquet of Praises for My KING
2. Christian Jokes for the Serious Religious' Folks!
3. Jesus Healed You!
4. Praise24Ever! (also in Tamil version)
5. The 5G Network of GOD
6. Building Faith over F.E.A.R- FACE EVERYTHING AND RISE with JESUS
7. Hebrew and Greek Praise and Worship Words
8. Godly Mothers' and Grandmothers' Bible Story time for Kids!
9. Miracles of Jesus in Pictures
10. Raise your Praise all 365 Days
11. Thanking GOD with an Attitude of Gratitude
12. Meditating on the Attributes of GOD
13. Puppet Scripts
14. Alcohol Ruins, JESUS Reforms, Renews & Restores!
15. Habakkuk 2:2 Christian Daily Journal, Planner & Organizer
16. ABC of GOD's Word for Handwriting Practice
17. Daily Bible Verse Handwriting Practice (Building Godly Character & Faith through Cursive Handwriting Practice!)
18. Guiding Light: Fun & Faith-Building Bible Activities for Children
19. Rejecting Grasshopper Talk: From Grasshopper to Giant-Killer-*Defeating Giants Daily!*
20. Teen Titans of Faith: *Building Courage, Determination & Christ-like-Esteem*
21. I AM Empowered: *Unleashing Divine Power with Positive Declarations*
22. Be A Solution Provider-*From Passion to Purpose*: *A Biblical Guide to Being the Answer to the World!*
23. Miracles of JESUS
24. Parables of Jesus for a Meaningful Life!
25. A Grateful Heart: Importance of Sharing Testimonies of GOD's Grace
26. Melodies of Worship to JESUS: 31 Songs of Praise & Worship From My Heart to HIS!
27. I AM SO BLESSED!
28. My Daily Cup of Energizer
29. 31 Leadership Lessons *from* Jesus- *The Supreme*

Leader
30. Peace Amidst Storms: A Biblical Guide to Conquering
    S.T.R.E.S.S.
31. Rise Above: 20 Biblical Eagle Lessons for Life's
    Triumphs
32. Godly Goal Setting: *The FAITHFUL Blueprint for a
    Purpose-Driven Life*
33. The Profound Attributes of our Mighty GOD:
    Understanding the 10S's of the Almighty
34. Worship Now, Worship Forever: *A Journey from Earthly
    Praise to Eternal Glory*

Besides regularly contributing to business & trade journals, including international ones such as the 'Creative Training Techniques' and the 'Sales News' of the U.S.A, He is also a member of several prestigious bodies & trade associations, having participated in many Conferences & Workshops in India & Overseas.

Prior to his last assignment of leading & managing a large MNC as head, Gerard had a 3-year stint in the Middle East as a Consultant with a leading British Consultancy Firm.

As the past 'Official Country Representative' for the International Business Award- 'THE STEVIES'-(the business world's own Oscar) for about 4 years- he ensured a few Indian companies that qualify for the same every year!

Gerard can be contacted at:
Email: training@Sales-Training.in,training@CollectionSkills.com
Websites:

www.Sales-Training.in
www.EtiquetteWorks.in
www.CollectionSkills.com
www.RetailSalesTraining.in
www.SalesTrainingIndia.com
www.ManualPreparation.com
www.TrainingWithPuppets.com
www.FirstContactAcademy.com
www.SalesAndMarketingRecruiter.com

Our TRAININGS that can help your team

- ✓ **Sales Effectiveness**: Selling Skills for any Sector: Service/ Logistics/ FMCG Realty/ Insurance & Finance/ Media/ SPA's, Health Clubs & Salons/ Key Account Management, Effective Negotiation Skills/ Bid & Proposal Management Skills/ Retail Sales Training: Any Sector (Auto, Jewelry, Clothing, Luxury etc)
- ✓ **Customer Service Skills**-Complaints Handling & Customer Retention
- ✓ **Debt Prevention & Collection Skills**
- ✓ **Etiquette & Grooming**
- ✓ **Leadership & Managerial Skills**
- ✓ **Self & Personal Development Skills**: Presentation Skills/ Effective Communication Skills/Business Proposal Writing Skills/ Problem Solving & Decision Making Skills/ Empowering Secretaries-The perfect PA! (For Secretaries & PA's)/ Effective Time Management/ Teamwork & Teambuilding/ P.R.I.D.E- **P**ersonal **R**esponsibility **I**n **D**elivering Excellence

www.ingramcontent.com/pod-product-compliance
Lightning Source LLC
LaVergne TN
LVHW020937200726

843506LV00011B/2050